DOGBOY

David McGimpsey

Dogboy

ECW PRESS

CANADIAN CATALOGUING IN PUBLICATION DATA

McGimpsey, David, 1962–
Dogboy

Poems.

ISBN 1-55022-355-0

I. Title.

PS8575.G48D63 1998   C811'.54   C98-930257-1
PR9199.3.M33D63 1998

Edited for the press by Michael Holmes.

Cover design and artwork by Gordon Robertson.
Author photo by John Fraser.
Imaging by ECW Type & Art, Oakville, Ontario.
Printed by AGMV Marquis Imprimeur, Cap-Saint-Ignace, Quebec.

Distributed in Canada by General Distribution Services,
30 Lesmill Road, Don Mills, Ontario M3B 2T6.

Published by ECW PRESS,
2120 Queen Street East, Suite 200,
Toronto, Ontario M4E 1E2.

www.ecw.ca/press

Table of Contents

3 /

4 /

5 /

Acknowledgements

These poems (or different forms of them) have appeared, or will appear, in *Quarry*, *Spitball*, *Event*, CBC *Sunday Morning*, *Canadian Literature*, *Fortnight*, *Booglit*, *The Pottersfield Portfolio* and *Pudding Magazine*.

Grateful thanks to John Bennett, Alicia Boutilier, April Bulmer, John Fraser, Michael Holmes, Scott Macdonald, Karen Massey, Dick Miller, Nick and Bernadette Mount. To Gail August; to Lynn, Jim, Mary, Heather and Doug Crosbie; to my sister Janice; to my parents John and Mary; to my wife Carol.

To my brothers Johnny & Mike

I

BUTTER-FLAVORED CIGARETTES

Just pretend I'm on the CBC
saying things that can't be cancelled
even if they aren't particularly filled
with words like *euphonious* or *recyclable*

I'm talking about spending spring near my fridge
and giving money to save the elks
and I'm going to start working for work's sake
within the big plastic frank called Weenieworld.

Doesn't it bring back memories
of the summer I trashed your car
and complained you weren't "supportive"?
Doesn't my voice sound all sexy?

Just pretend I'm on the vibraphone
and I've had all my daily essential rums —
the sound is woofing through,
you say it's like winter but you know it's like *wow*.

I, URKEL

You were first-year college and so was I.
You took European languages
and seriously asked Prof. Corcova
what the Spanish word for "garter" is —
so you let me mentally unsnap your *jarretera*
and told me again and again
that doesn't make us boyfriend and girlfriend.
I didn't understand, but when you moved in
with that guy named Stefan it was pretty clear
and I slipped back onto the grey El that brought me here.

This can not be me, my sweet little potato puff.

You were a sophomore and I was at my labs,
malt stains on my coat, hardly talking anymore;
the loneliness had settled inside me and into extra weight.
You would hardly recognize the meaty geek
who feels like nothing will ever get done.

(And I no longer looked for you around campus.)

On the weekends I invented a device that
automatically ripens avocados;
I devised a system for the pleasant transmission
of cornet sounds to soothe professional sports crowds
and, unfortunately,
I also contracted a condition known as *bumblefoot*
which heretofore was limited to penguins in captivity —
and once, by accident, I ate twenty dollars worth of stamps.

Rumor was you were still around,
playing the college girl, dressing well enough

to dare silver clothes every now and then;
sharing fashion-crime jokes with all the Jennifers
who whispered behind your back
that you too were a little *old* for this.

I wanted to make some remark about us one day —
some little snippet that would contain a dramatic word
like *provenance* or *enamorada*
and it would tell you everything that's happened
in the bald summers since the bad old days.
But, well after the unattended reunions —
when I no longer knew
why you looked the way you do —
in the best stretch of the summer,
I saw you in an old wooden phonebooth
at one of those tacky bars around Rush and Division Streets.
You looked like a billboard athlete;
purple crush shorts, an orange headband.
I vibrated with emotion:
all those years suddenly collapsed inside me
and all my exterior resolve fell
into the fault line of a great quake.

If only I could step into a transformation chamber
and emerge as somebody I used to be.
If only I could speak that other language
you once so desperately wanted to hear.
But I turned away and ordered something soft —
if you had the middle-aged grace
to come up to me and just say hello
I was ready to say, in my best, deepest voice
*You must have me confused with somebody else —
maybe my brother!*
and ask for a cigarette before walking away.

Brands of Coffee/Literary Terms

Nescafé

Catharsis

Nabob

Ab Ovo

Taster's Choice

Terza Rima

Maxwell House

Mock Epic

Folger's

Faustian

Sanka

Haiku

Blue Mountain Blend

Black Mountain Poets

Encore

Brands of Detergent/Deadly Sins

Tide

Envy

Bold

Lust

Dash

Gluttony

Gleam

Wrath

Cheer

Greed

Mr. Clean

Sloth

Palmolive

Pride

LI'L CAMILLAGATE

She's my diesel-fume darling
riding the bus to work with her everyday.

But every now and then she wants to be overheard.
Because she wants somebody to hear
because God knows I'm not listening anymore.
"Princess Diana was a pig" she says,
and nothing stirs; she waits for a reaction.
The bus jolts and speeds past laundromats and bars.
(Why are there so many laundromats in this city?
It never struck me as that spectacularly clean.)
Nothing stirs: she is educated and well-liked.
I think of a newspaper full of citytime listings:
Italian horror movies; 50s-style burlesque, pasties twirling;
and anti-Castro all-Cuban AA meetings.
Of course, she is going to say it again.
The bus limps into center lane traffic,
the driver's sunglasses reflects our faces.
"A god-damn pig" comes each syllable
with muddied attention, no longer concerned
about Diana and how many,
exactly how many stops are left.

GOUDAMUNDO

Hamlet walks up to Ophelia and says
"What did you do with that video? The one
where Fonzie tells everybody to wake up
and for a moment they do." Ophelia weeps
"I didn't touch your stupid videos,"
and she slams the door. From the other side
she recites a poem about wild weekends
and the regrets of the dim workplace.
Hamlet rewinds, curses the neighbors
and cues up his very favorite scenes.
"I lived for an afternoon well beyond"
she says in her lost country girl voice,
while her prince looks through the cool tokens
of Wisconsin's ruined castles of cheese.

THE FLY, MFA

My bile is mutating, sweetheart
and I'm not cursing —
I'm just pointing it out:
my fist has not yet gone through the window.
Can I show you my mutations?

My days as a moth-like thing,
a pupal crouton destined for the plates
of eccentric societies who sauté butterflies
and wrap ants in chocolate coating.
I was once that crunchy.

It had something to do with moving,
a series of mutterings at the lab,
and my failure to file federal income tax.
Next thing you know I've got hair on my back
and nothing's what it used to be.

It isn't spilt milk or guilty pudding:
you see in my glossy photo
my unreachable insectoid despair,
all the things you'd want in a half-man.
My transformed microscopic thing,
my miracle scientist's petri dish *oops*
is a groovy kind of larval wiggle.

On the cover of *Time* you can see my fillings.
Inside, there's a picture of my dentist,
who boasts in a byline,
        "I sense an improved person."
No smudgy newsprint fingertips
with that magazine;
fantasize —
no angry smudges, sugar.

ONE MAN BAND

Things just haven't been the same
Since Billy Ray Cyrus faded away
And I lost my job taking care
Of his ugly-assed pony-tail.

And things took a turn for the worse
When I went to the Welfare dressed as a clown
And I took a nap at the feet of the associate undersecretary
To the liaison to the Finance Minister.

But I'm full of sunshine and smiles
Because I've stolen about 40 dollars worth of subway tokens
I've got a pocket full of licorice bits
I'm a one man band.

I used to have a girl
Who went by the stage name of "Monique"
But she left me when I told her
I was kind of in love with her shoes.

So I write another letter to Kathie Lee
And tell her that if I ever win the lottery
I'm going to buy a car and spend the rest
on Kenny Rogers' chicken
    (you got to know when to hold 'em).

But I'm full of sunshine and smiles
Because I've finally found a way to shave my back
I've got a bag of complimentary popcorn from Jumbo Video
I'm a one man band.

What if God Was Wilford Brimley?

On the seventh day he'd loosen his suspenders.

He'd see the lakeshore ripples in daylight
colored by the surrounding maple trees
and he'd be happy with what he's done for awhile.

But we would feel his wrath
as co-dependency meetings
and the scent of Calvin Klein's "Escape"
comes to the tractor towns of Vermont.
The line from *Newhart* would go:
"This is my brother Satan
and this is my other brother Satan."

And we'd all be saying,

> Where were you Brimley?
> When the darkness rushed through me?
> When I saw death claim all?
> When death claimed me like a cheap Midway prize?
> Brimley,
> why did you make people
> sweet as donut glaze
> and sharp as an X-acto?

But we are again reminded of the Commandments.
One of them now being, "eat thou plenty of oatmeal."

And let's face it,
this divine directive might be more helpful
than the notoriously problematic
"thou shalt have no other gods before me,"
to say nothing of the one about adultery.

Bowl by bowl we'd wake
to the smallness of our disappointments
and to a brief sweetness
(in low-fat righteousness)
pleasing to the belly
that trembles the heavens.

SING ALONG JUBILEE

Nobody ever sang along.
Nobody ever hummed away
with the Ottawa Valley Melodeers.
No matter where they were,
no matter how deep into the soup,
no matter how lost in winter;
among lost wool hats in the snow
in the browned suburban slop,
nobody ever sang along
unless they had some secret thing
in the warmth of their basements
of orange furniture
and freestanding ashtrays
where everything was possible:
Tommy Hunter kisses Bryan Adams
and all is right with the world.

The *Jubliee* people would always promise
Anne Murray would be along next week,
and next week Anne wouldn't show
and they would promise again.
And each week their promises grew more desperate,
their apologies more sincere —
there was a musicality in that.

Gordon Lightfoot sang:
    "In the early morning rain
    my granny went insane
    she bought a yellow snowmobile
    and moved to central Florida"
but we didn't sing along, no matter how much they said we did.

Say what you will about the Rita MacNeil / Geddy Lee duets
the silence was deafening,
but the learning is certain:

When you think a Stan Rogers song
actually expresses your personal experiences
it is time to leave Nova Scotia.

"My Name is Kimmy G."

I had no idea she wrote poetry. She certainly didn't say anything about it on the train to her meeting. It's only now, when it's too late, that I've realized K's writing was maybe the only thing holding her together. She was like that: never revealing herself and maybe that was part of her problem with the group. I'm not even certain I listened to her read it that night. I remember sitting there, drinking tea out of a styrofoam cup, eager to get back on the train. I asked her for a copy and she laughed in that angry way of hers and said there were no copies and no title yet, but it would make her happy if I saved the original for her. Considering everything that's happened, I hope I've done the right thing submitting it for publication.

— Anonymous

I backtrack through the conversations
remembering even the missed expressions
what's that word? when you won't go outside?
and pretend to forget how I promised
to not ride the stationary bicycle when I was "at it"
and to be extra careful when I got on the phone.

Let's not, let's not.
What are you thinking? what are you thinking?
Not now, not now.
Just tell me, why can't you tell me?

So I took up the piano
and learned to sing the potato's song
if only I could sleep for awhile.
Did you know, even in the depths of my "sadness,"
I invented a famous, slovenly cocktail:

The Gin Gibbler, that frozen
lemon lime thing with the jalapeño finish, is mine —
and it's still my proudest achievement
even if it's "virgin gibblers" from now on.

The piano keys melted away, of course,
and I started to wear lycra and poly-knits
and stopped looking at the mirror
(having a good idea who would look back).
Exhausted by imaginary love affairs
meant to spell the sadnesses of ab work,
telephone bills, engagement parties,
love was crushed creatively.
I can't tell you anything
because I can't tell you anything.
I'd try and look to the Bible for guidance
but I always came across some severe
Old Testament admonition about *fools*
which gave me just enough juice
to get back to the country and western:

> *If I told you the truth*
> *and said I was a liar back then*
> *would you believe me*
> *or the girl I used to be?*

I remember the lyrics so well,
maybe it wasn't such a surprise
I did OK at SF State.
All tea, bones and *no thank you*:
I drew a circle around my talent
so I could just sit at my spinet,
tilt my head back
and drift from the old pals
who would just bring more beautiful children

to beautiful Sunnyvale;
who would never write back
because of something I said or did.
Cheers!
I hate it when you get like that.
It's all written down somewhere
every bold and lovely lie —
I promise, I promise,
I'll change, I'll change.
Sometimes,
I wish I could neatly fold myself
and be forgotten
and all my words
would lose their stings and comforts
and become just paper:
inoffensively lost in the stacks
of old xeroxes, catalogues
and *things to do today.*

— Aug. 29, 1996 San Francisco

2

Chubby Chased

When I got to my self-esteem workshop
the group-leader was sitting there in the dark
eating Oreos, and he looked up and said "I guess
you'll be wanting some of these — eh, tubby?"

I would have complained and asked for my money back
but if I could do something like that
why would I be spending my Wednesday nights
at the Community Center, learning more about smoking cigarettes?

Her name was Patricia and we met up later at Starbucks.
She insulted the way I dressed
but was fascinated with the way I drooped
when I admitted I buy all my clothes at Wal-Mart.

We pitched our pup tent in middle America
and got away from the city, but not the Kraft macaroni.
I said "Trish, do you remember that workshop I was in?
God, was I ever a ring-ding to think that would make a difference."

LOCKLEAREAN DELUSIONS

I thought I was one of Amanda's stock-room boys
but it turned out I just took too much Benadryl
and that I was all nutso in a West Hollywood bar
crying and screaming "please read my script please."

Oh, as Amanda's stock boy I stocked and stocked
like for *hours* — she knew what she was doing
and I was certain she was talking dirty to me
but it turned out I was just insulting an old friend

talking to her like she was out to get me
saying, "you hate my script don't you? don't you?"
until she left and I smashed something expensive
and got tossed and mumbled evensong and fell asleep outside.

I will cherish the scars the sunburn has left
and I will start to call myself *Repulso The Magician*
for all the pretty things I've disappeared from,
lips-first by the Wilshire Courtyard.

Nova Smoked Blubber

Once you consider getting married in your K-Way jackets
it's time to leave Chilliwack;
we thought we were a healthy version of Sid and Nancy,
but were more like a protein-deficient Rod Taylor and Doris Day.

So we headed east and east some more
until the desperation of our resolve was deeply felt —
we were bound for Musquodoboit,
where the silly mackerel meet the happy smelt.

We hammered together a shack
and puttered quietly through the wallpapering stage,
listening out the window for the roar of the sea,
and to hear the mullahs weep for *Ozzie and Harriet*.

My sweet Orenthalena,
we've told each other enough white lies to clothe Wimbledon
and now it's like we'll never get out of here —
and never, ever, have I felt so utterly blue and Gilligonian.

King Kamehamayonnaise

Oceans away with all their cold blackness
how they say so little except *get away*;
how warm the ankles feel so frozen —
oceans so deadly in our dumpy backyard.

Wicked landscape tattoos on my private places:
I've altered my outsides and insides for you,
hollowed my diary into a recipe book
and called myself *M. Bouftout* just for laughs.

The Pacific wind is at my stomach
early on and it stabs at me —
my spideysense tells me it won't be long, then
you come up like Poseidon,

lassoing me with columns and cancers —
intensifying every thing I never bothered to learn —
feels like an Antarctic getaway —
E-Z savings, looks good 4-Ever.

ROAD ROAST (RUMP)

She said I'd never die from self-doubt
and I couldn't think of much to say to that
but I thought about it as my knees gave way
and I collapsed right there on Sunset Blvd. in front of *BookSoup.*

I remember the heat of the sun on my neck
and twisting my head from the impressive footwear
of passersby and the horrible, yellow brightness of the billboards —
O God, I felt so horribly out-of-State.

I could hear the off-ramp Platters sing
That's the way it is in Loserville.
We're a demented but proud and gated community
that will not let the winners in.

In bed, I heard from my agent, she just called to say
I had said no to her for the very last time.
i.e. "You'll be waiting to be an extra in a *Jim* Hanks vehicle
in between fainting spells on the boulevard."

PHD WITH PERFECT PH BALANCE

Long before you could waste your life on-line,
before Toronto theatre, before the phrase
"The best thing from Marisa Tomei since *My Cousin Vinny*"
I would sit in my office and fall apart.

Once, a kid with a strange football injury
told me to "sit up" and take his complaints "like a man."
Oh, I tried, said "un-hunh" a lot and wondered
what I'd miss more if I gave up, the disdain or the contempt?

I'd take the subway uptown in the evenings,
working the day in my head till I sounded like a brave Ulsterman;
my limp comb-over unravelling with sleep,
always missing my stop, not knowing where I was.

The footballer went on to write more books than me,
even claimed he had sex with Sylvia Plath —
he wrote: "She was going ooo-wee like some hillbilly chick."
We all have some business to take care of.

THE ELVIS AWARDS

The way Marcia Brady grew and grew
and sang de-alcoholized country on PBS
I'm so happy to have just held onto my old shoes
to sing along and say unto you, I am no different.

Don't think I'm unmoved:
I've given up two solid hours of TV per day
and have big plans to shed the remaining ten —
isn't that something, my Jesu with the ale-soaked eyes?

Looks like you'll be seeing a little too much of me,
goofy-girl with hair like corn flakes.
I can make a pudding out of rejection slips,
I can put my state in two words (de pressed),

but the envelopes, please. *Let it be me.*
The most auspicious weight gain? *Let it be me.*
The best concealment of a percodan addiction? *Let it be me.*
The most garbled expression of devotion? *O! Let it be me!*

LUMPY LOU

Lumpy Lou de Loup Garou
Had a book of jingles called *Boo Hoo Hoo*
He cried a little cry, sighed a little sigh,
And Lord he felt like having another piece of pie.

Now Fifi Lafitte from the county Mesquite
Had a home in the hills and size ten feet
She sobbed a little sob, blubbered *blub blub blub*
Then moved to Lafayette in search of love.

She met Lumpy Lou in a stinky bayou,
Said she knew every word of *Boo Hoo Hoo*
It made her wail, it made her drink,
It made her attempt to unclog the sink.

"Would you like some pie?" Lou said to Ms. Lafitte
"It's made of bog and sod and authentic Irish peat."
Fifi cried *"oui"* and Lumpy Lou cried "hoo-ee"
As they dined *à deux* over the muddy, muddy treat.

O'BEANER

She started telling me an "old Irish tale"
about a smelly blackthorn pin,
but as soon as I heard the word "Irish"
I thought of the day I got loaded at Sullivan's Tap Room.

God, that was a tall-bottled Boston adventure,
but it did not quite bring us up to the next feature;
our little movie has become predictable
but we're aggressively selling the amiable soundtrack.

Darling, there's a chartbuster somewhere,
whether Kennedy or Knievel, whose lyrics never fade.
I finally said she should enter that one in a short story contest,
but she was against all such competitions,

claiming she was once *Miss Sudafed* —
and although I can attest to a determined sleepiness,
a certain inability to operate heavy machinery,
I never quite saw the tell-tale tiara.

It's The Diet Pills Talking

She waltzed into K-Mart with her last cheque,
and came out with enough socks for a lifetime —
as God was her witness,
she would never go sock-hungry again.

Well-hosed and fond of the stuff in cans,
I called her Lola but she called me "the quitter."
Anyway, I stole her stepfather's Pinto
and it exploded while I was in a bordello in Escanaba, Michigan.

In the u.p. (as the natives call it) I settled down
and worked as a short order cook at the local Days Inn.
Mountains of fries passed the time,
but oh how I missed the way she made plans to leave me.

Lola-baby, nobody pukes up blood like your little cabbage —
and when I'm all warped-out on ginseng root
I feel like a million tubers
lighting the road back to you and your new job.

Love Me, Love Kathie Lee

I'd be paying more attention
but the cola wars are raging inside my head
and I have some really close friends outside the county,
who are having a really big party, so buh-bye.

L'amour is in the bungalow
and I'm sending my tax rebate back into the economy.
"What would you say if someone said you drink too much?"
"Mind your own business, son."

I stride on stage and I'm saying
you hate me, you really hate me
when the award is in my hand —
which way was that terrific party? Is this it?

They sing of exotic birds, rarely in the city,
who fly into skyscraper windows full bore,
looking to penetrate the bright office lights;
and there we are on the sidewalk at dawn we are.

BLUE PLATE LARDCAKE

The old yearbook in all its hairy glory
has no notice of the little tremors I would experience;
the hotel rooms and nightmarescapes of the West Island —
never the Kevin Arnold, always the Nelson Muntz.

No recollection of the collection plates eyed
and all the wee chapbooks and articles
whose publication caused my friends
a lifetime of embarrassment (if only they were published,

if only I had friends). Back you go to the nostalgia pit
full of sweat, misgivings and Styx lyrics
down in the depths of the Loserville Mall,
where I talk of the Fetish Café in downtown Montreal.

Oh, you remember what I meant
and I didn't mean what I meant because what I mean
suddenly needs to be hammered down
by the food fair where the valedictorians work.

TUBBYROTICA

The doctor asked me to say something I liked about myself
so I said I was "proud of all the vigorous flossing"
and she smiled broadly, folded her notebook,
exhaled and softly asked "water?"

I didn't go for the drink and waved by the receptionist.
When I was on Second Avenue
I was thirsty for something else altogether
lost again in a platter of buffalo-schnitzel.

Oh, the mai tais were cold, cold, cold,
and I was feeling like Ted Danson with a new wig,
and I was telling this college girl about my afternoons
and she said "gosh, how can you afford all those sessions?"

So there we were arguing underneath the track lighting
and I thought this was it, we could be the Taster's Choice couple,
too busy for television, too bold for the subway —
oh, I should've said yes to that glass of water.

EL NOODLE

Golden warthogs fill your eyes;
stamped, self-addressed envelopes enclosed inside,
return near the propitious sniff of the canal,
Irish as Tom Cruise and all small inside.

Like everybody, I work for a living,
and, like some, not always that hard.
Example: my notes featuring "she put the xxx in Xmas
and it was time to hang up the stockings."

No longer a Katie Couric feel-good piece,
I've gone over to the Geraldodome;
home of the beekeepers' daughters
and the free-agents whose indolent swings make millions.

I'm onto something, I have struck something, you say
(something besides the ability to sound dumb
by repeatedly writing the phrase "you say"?),
but I'm just sitting there like week-old meatloaf soup.

OBLADIOBLAHATEMYLIFE

Word was he was coming a little unhinged;
when he sang the Beatles "All You Need is Love"
he'd go with the lyrics "I Really Wish I Was Dead"
and he wasn't even bothering to keep the tune.

He was more than a friend, he was an idiot pal —
I owed the guy, so I wrote him a concerned note,
full of suggested readings I thought separate the blue from the suicidal,
and he wrote back on looseleaf paper spotted with orange soda stains:

"Thanks, but I think I've developed an intolerance to those nutrients:
sure, it would taste great, but I'll spend weeks fighting it back.
Now, all I can seem to handle is the *Archie with Jughead Digest*,
and, lately, I'm getting terribly disquieted with Arch."

So the amateur left the grand old game to the pro,
but just when I was about to get my own life in order,
I flopped face-first in springtime mud
and the words bubbled up to the sky,
        "you are so right, buddy-boy, I hear you, I hear."

THE PLUMPEST PLANET

Jupiter is in the house and it radiates hope
as the summer winds begin to switch
and shake my acne scars until my face aches
with the gone "poetry" of our early twenties.

I used to imitate Petrarch,
now I just remember our trip to Daytona Beach —
I was luckier than Lyle Lovett and happier
than Boris Yeltsin in a basement full of potatoes.

Somebody told me of how you went to Alberta
and your wheat-blonde sense of loss was lost
and you don't ever write or ever write back
since you misunderstood my inquiry about *the special sauce.*

Jupiter holds the hammer, Calpurnia sweet,
some star will shine through and break my forehead
and the Bizarro-world me will rise through
to once again karaoke *The Summer Wind.*

FLABTASTICO

Furniture stain removal by moonlight
and you never said a word —
it was never about me and the telephone
or how dumb I sounded defending myself.

You said "I have to brush"
and in the cold gravity of your stoop
I thought you were a supermodel brain surgeon
and that we'd share our share of poor homonyms.

It's not like you wouldn't recognize me today.
You haven't scattered that far —
even though you're on the radio saying
I am Bob Packwood's brother.

That night, I picked at paint chips on the beams
while I heard the sink running
and running until I realized
you'd locked the door behind you.

Ho-Do

I wasn't surprised by the bad reports the manager wrote
(except by her repetition of the word "drowsy")
and when I left the main office I proclaimed
this was my Independence Day, sort of, kind of, I guess.

All of a sudden in the brightness of the afternoon
I thought of the night I wanted to just hold your hand
but instead I told you of my bout
with the hot-dog disease *listeria*.

I'm home by 3 and dead under the kitchen table
thinking my lackey is coming by with Cybill Shepherd
and she'll say something witty about the night
and we will forget it all as we move out to the Valley.

Oh, I'll get back to the hot-links, just you wait,
you may have plans to marry, you may even have a job;
but my rut will have its charms, its lava lamps,
and its own football-pitch-wide frankfurter casseroles.

CONGRATULATIONS, LOSER

She thought she'd be sweet and all *let's-stay-friends*,
calling after a couple of weeks,
from *that* place, to ask if I was "eating all right."
I said "That all depends, baby; is aspirin a food?"

She hung up. *Everybody wants to be*
further from me. And I know the song:
Closer to Free is not inscribed on many friendship rings,
and I don't recall ever wanting it inside mine.

Back in the day she pledged she was going to own
every corner of this pigstink town,
but now, she'll just settle for the charms
of the stock-room boy.

Check out my gray hair! Check it out!
Have you ever seen such a furry old ash can?
O! Yes! Every woman has a fantasy
and lately I do not resemble one.

Won't You Take Me To Stinkytown?

Before you'd admit you wouldn't do any better than me
it was like we were at El Alamein,
fighting over the unlikely terrain with mouthfuls of dust:
I'm OK *but who the hell are you!*

So, here I am, the reconstructed Air Supply fan
taking my work onto the early morning trains,
passing lumber yards and fast food chains, oh,
let's remarry in the chapel and call our daughter "Loopy."

You still have the sex appeal of an AAA-member —
always knowing what to do in case of emergency.
And so was our lusty Miada hoodoo:
tracing the soft shoulders of the Heritage Highway,

all the way through the counties around Long Sault, Ontario,
where the perch rolls at the *Perch Palace* glisten
and shame the bad name once given to mercury,
and where we could settle and get so *hot hot hot.*

Hail to the Beef

Let's get the story straight: Al Gore was talking to my crew
and he used the phrase "a few displaced foresters,"
but I thought he said "you disgraceful losers."
The rest is videoclips you've seen a million times.

Locked alone, alone, the ghost of William Henry Taft
has been emanating from my mashed potatoes
saying I've been a wicked li'l gravy-boy
and I'll never be free to enjoy all of life's tiddlyumpums.

But like all the one-syllable Presidents —
Polk, Pierce, Grant, Hayes, Ford, Bush — even the ghost-Taft
wasn't worth listening to. No wonder everybody passed
so heartily on Dole and, no doubt, Gore — oh, I'll be vindicated.

I stare through my private window and I dare to dream:
one day my RV will command the wooded roads that lead
to Branson, Missouri and its comedians whose punchlines
always end with "ain't that there the truth ain't it?"

I AM PRODUCE-BOY

It's true, when you work a grocery store cash
you can tell what people are like by the food they buy,
but when you've been working the cash for 10 years
who gives a shit what people are really like?

I took to poetry and working the floor,
writing verse on overripe pumpkins and melons,
things about my co-workers — delightful gambols
I liked to call "softi-freeze pantaloon dramas."

I dreamed of the big time and of old New England,
and kept at it until the manager brought me in the office
because I once ate a pina colada-scented candle. I said:
"You can't fire me, I'm fat, — I mean, I quit!"

Yes, writing free verse is like playing tennis with Robert Frost,
your overhand smash dings off his racket at 100 mph —
and gets him square in the nose: blood everywhere
at the Middlebury Golf and Tennis Club.

I win! I win!

THE FAT OPRAH POLKA

I thought of dying with a potion
but eating turnip is enough,
thought of diving before the subway
if I could no longer overstuff,

thought of writing in a diary
about how even watching TV was too much,
but it was time to go up and down to the sounds
of the Fat Oprah Polka.

Run for miles, run for miles,
hope the pity never stops.
Do your flexes, do your crunches,
but do not lick the pot.

Deep-fried gouda is a no-no,
but you can gorge on old kumquats.
Girls and boys (but not that many boys),
Love the Fat Oprah Polka.

Good Olestra Goodness

Times are tough out here on Thanksgiving Day.
I just went to the grocery store and there was Juan Valdez
with a handpainted sign that read "cheap donkey meat"
and *Señor V* was making a fair bit of cash.

I spend this holiday as I spend all others,
with a videotape jam-packed full of episodes of *T.J. Hooker*,
a jar of mayonnaise and a big wooden spoon.
I'm not looking forward to Christmas.

Sometimes, it's like I can barely get up to take my sleeping pills.
Whenever I resolve to do something about my state
I do something like sign up for a non-credit jujitsu class
but stay in to write angry letters to Burt Reynolds instead.

I thought I'd break out the cranberry molds this year
and get all hearthy and sweater-sexy on health food,
but here, under the provincial mists of downsizing,
health food means boasting "our beef is now larva-free."

POUBELLERIE

One second you're all tequila shooters
falling asleep in each other's arms
singing *Ku-u-i-po* and still tasting the lime and salt
all the way through the simple ceremony.

Then it's all "don't tell me, don't tell me!"
and "damn it, you're just like your father!"
while you're picking at crumbs stuck to the tablespread,
lifting your eyes to see if *Murder, She Wrote* is on.

First, you're all *let's take the phone off the hook*
and watch Valerie Bertinelli movies together,
eating slowly and with good humor at the very worst restaurants,
never really caring about what's out there.

Next thing you know you're both earnestly
paying attention to the words in the runaway bestseller
Men Are From Mars, Women Are From Venus,
screaming "honey, where's my godamned highlighter?"

Stump Professor Stumpy

When my students were spelling things out loud
because they thought I wouldn't understand
I figured my career as a teacher was in trouble,
so I bought *Teaching for Dummies* and underlined like crazy.

Getting young adults to "ask the right questions" was the key,
and every afternoon I tried and tried
but, unfortunately, the only question they asked was,
"Sir, do you, like, *own* a mirror?"

Now I've been trying to take up smoking.
I'm afraid I may be the only person in the world
who lacks the will-power to *start* the habit.
But I think of those disappointed kids and inhale deeply.

I don't care for the nicotine, but you gotta love the tar.
And here's something else you won't learn in school:
The secret ingredient in American cigarettes?
Little chocolate marshmallows.

WAYNE NEWTON'S THEORY OF GRAVITY

I took my Dad to Vegas to celebrate his successful surgery
and to get away from my difficult second year of "regular payments."
"What are we doing here?" Pops would say
as if he wasn't having the greatest time in his whole damn life.

I had a little too much of the bright lights (if you know what I mean)
and cooled my luck by taking the old man
to a feverish circus show where, sadly,
he was mauled by a toothless stage lion named "Barry."

In the ambulance, the ambulance guy said
"Sometimes cats can tell when something's wrong,"
so I said "They always seem to know when to piss in my clothes"
and Pops angrily croaked, "couldn't you just sing something?"

"Uh, the cat and the bladder and the sophomore swoon,
Little white pills and divorced by June.
When I get my cheque, Dad, I'll get new clothes —
You know it's on the government then, Dad,
        You know it's on the government then."

LITTLE SQUIBBER

All fix-it-upper gearheadedness grinds me down:
I plan on making it through my life
without ever sanding a floor
without ever saying "I think it's the alternator"

without ever installing a new sprinkler system
and without ever buying a brand new riding mower.
The folds of my neck turned funny colors by the sun
turning to my neighbor to say "ain't she a beaut?"

Needless to say these proud designs
dovetail from my less boastworthy fates
to never have a chequing account
to never have an insurance claim pay off

and to momentarily consider taking
my neighbor's empties away for the deposit money
so I could go where they always know your name
as long as your name is *Buddy*.

HANDY HINTS FOR YOUR PRESS KIT

You can't say "testicle" on television.
You shouldn't address David Gilmour as "punkin."
And don't, in your grant application forms, admit to fantasies
involving "an angry Silken Laumann and a wet oar."

Remember, if the FBI has commended
your obsessed fan letters to Justine Bateman
for their "flawless grammar and extensive use of footnotes"
this is not like winning the Lampert award.

Even if CSIS has said more or less the same thing
about your correspondence with the late Bruno Gerussi
the Canadian content will not get you up to the podium
so you can blow kisses to Keith Spicer.

You can't say "I'm all sloppy with discount vodka"
on early morning TV (even if you are), and please,
you shouldn't ever tell me I smell like Cap'n Crunch
because I have feelings too, Chester.

Too Much Slouching,
Not Enough Slumping

I loved her but she made me forgo my plans
to become an airport minister:
those little bibles and those little vodka bottles
always in my linty, gabardine pockets.

The good lord helped me metabolize
but she made me check into a Minnesota clinic,
forcing me to go under an assumed name.
I picked the unlikely sobriquet "McGimpsey."

What kind of name is that?
I told everybody it was all things European,
and that I came from a long line of paprika millers
and disreputable computer salesmen.

And sooner rather than later I felt better anyway —
ain't it funny how butter melts away —
she made sure when she said she was off to T.O.
I could *feel* each little syllable.

LEAVING VIVA LAS VEGAS

When the *Up With People* people voted me
the guy most likely to die a miserable death,
you stood up to the crowded, smokeless theatre
to say "when push came to shove" I was an ox.

You made me luckier than Lucky Jackson,
not that I paid your sweetness much mind
through lunches of cellophane-flavored wine
at my dreamy back-alley version of Nicky Blair's.

Elbowed back to remorsefulness, to the familiar pities,
to the old "Mom, Dad, guess who's moving back?"
I still daydreamed of that dancing University thing
as undeniably male destinies settled my waist and head.

I scream at the folks, play the records I played in high school,
full of peanut butter again, unlikely to date again,
but as fortunate as a guy who finds a doctor
who'll warn against a "harmful nicotine deficiency."

3

RON HUNT AT BAT

(In 1971, Montreal Expos second baseman Ron Hunt set the
Major League single-season record for being hit by a pitch, a
staggering 50 times.)

At the only restaurant in town
the jukebox went:
In the summer of '71
Ron Hunt had a way of getting it done
and you folded your arms
to remind me I'd never be forgiven
for stating the obvious,
for saying on the phone
"Don't you want to do this?
This?"

Sending me and my many smells
through knots of daydreams
to one dollar bleacher seats
in a tin origami-upfold known as Jarry Park.
There is no need to do this,
this:
your notes of smoothed oak caskets and dogs barking,
(luckily) far from my dreams
of pop-top gushings and letting Ron Hunt do the work;
only Ron Hunt could work this demi-monde to any effect:
each squiggle of the city,
each lamented spill,
each rationalized heart-drop of June —
it's all pasted in a spiral-bound scrap-book
like mementos of a confession gone wrong;
no, Father, I have not sinned.

It gets worse in verse, but,
as the *The Ron Hunt Book of Quotations* reads
"Otherwise, they might not know me for anything."

"I swear he likes it,"
a teammate said in *The World According to Ron Hunt*
after watching RH take
three practise beanballs from the pitching machine.
Ay yi.
As another disbelieving foe said in the second volume,
He's Ron Hunt and You're Not,
"He wasn't going to quit when he was obviously dead."

How all those words came to mean something to me.

When I came to your birthday party
for a ladle-full of clove soup
my head got so numb I didn't notice
the subtle desperations
and unspoken novellas of your little crowd;
sharing thoughts about John Travolta's thoughts on cloning,
about Timothy McVeigh's absent mother,
and whatever ever happened to Griffin O'Neal?
Oh, if Ti and Do
made it to the mothership in the tail of Hale-Bopp
would they be able to see their discarded vehicles
as they share their next stage laughs?
Could they remember the absorbed thuds of August,
the hamburgerhelper stink of our hands —
where there were Bacharachian promises, promises.

Thumbing the pages of *Ron Hunt in the Underworld*,
highlighting each brave embellishment,
I wonder if I could ever step into it
and take the pill wherever it hits,
because I am just as afraid as anybody —
and I pretend.
Hopped-up on *People* and *Movieline*
somewhere,
all Marilu Henner in a somersault,
monumental as Gary Cooper with his pants down.

We leave the only restaurant in town,
the tune still in our heads:
"It's not as easy as it seems
to take one for the team."
Setting out for the downtown core
far from Jarry, far from the Olympic Stadium:
the city I think about moving away from
every single day.
It's no good the way it is:
just imagine a super new development
where the super new ball park has it all inside:
the pity cakes, the fatigue dogs,
the pasta à la it's all over,
the sorbetti di not me not me.

MEDITATION AS DOM DIMAGGIO

Let the ball rest on the other side
until it recedes into the earth
and plumbs the volcanic streams below.
An obdurate rock
weighed only by the arcadian columns
in the *Sporting News*, once upon a summer ache,
a dot in the sky, a refracting pupil,
a thing that used to be so fat in the zone.

Even on the dust-jacket of my bio
you are bigger. Jolting out a hit,
your Frisco toe at my temple,
your eye on the ball.
I had some numbers but you had the hips.
Kid brother to the Clipper, Uncle Coffee,
I am a New England plastico man:
the industry is failing.

The knights of the keyboard out there
ask me for revelations of envy,
I tell them each afternoon was "swell,
real grass, real heroes."
Ya, like, I'm under your bitch-cloud.
Mistaken for you in the supermarket
I say *I am not Bramwell Brontë*
nor was I meant to be.

You are New York, I am Boston, I say.
That is, I'll play good ol' Dom in geek glasses
to your droopy-loner anyday.
At least I am not Vince
(but I have known his kind). He was 1st;
he gallantly flailed at big league pitches for 10 years
and then swallowed enough of the family name
to work door to door with his inferior eye.

You had the bonespurs a Marilyn could love;
you are a shadow with gristle deposits,
a ghost that smells of rye-seeped wool.
You leave a rose on her rock
everyday in California they say.
Sometimes I think an agent made it possible
and then I fall in my hands; I know better —
I knew what you could do long before High School.

All of us fish-sick in San Francisco,
capable of playing the outfield
or missing confession, drinking early beer.
I thought it would be me —
I am ashamed of how I sometimes feel
Othello-dizzy, lumped in heavy cottons,
around beds, desks, televisions — sour grapes:
calling you *dink* when the ad was on.

We did our thing for America-goes-to-war.
I believe, or told *The Globe* I believed
that batting records no longer mattered,
hadn't they heard of Hitler and Tojo?
The war was brief but there would be more noise:
the woo woo woo of those morons Simon and Garfunkel,
insect crackerjack stickball thieves —
"What's that you say Dom DiMaggio?"

The manufacturing base of New England has crumbled.
The Red Sox and Yankees do worse than the team from Toronto.
If the game lives or dies
Fenway Park will be tossed like a shoebox full of old bills.
The baseballs will no longer plop on Lansdowne,
fair game to the knees and elbows
of all the unpaying, opinionated fans
who can only afford to say "I got it."

Let the ball rest on the other side I say,
all the souvenirs will kill you.
Watch it go, applaud, curse, say bye-bye
but don't try to take it back.
I have no remarkable tan slacks to speak of,
nothing about the flecks of red in my eye.
I speak not of platinum but of plutonium,
something deep in the earth and best left whole.

ANOTHER EXPOEM, JULY 1990

As soon as we saw O'Neil's hit pass Wallach's glove
and dust the line above third base
we ran out of Riverfront;
we didn't (and just couldn't) see the celebratory fireworks
even though on the escalators to the parking level
we could hear.

Reds fans everywhere;
brought up in sunny Montreal,
not a single pennant velcroed to our wall;
all the way from Ville D'Anjou to see
the mighty Expos take their regular turn at failure.

A brutal sweep. *La balayage.*
3 days of abuse from Reds fans
who, in their first place brash intolerance,
were more like Mets fans than Mets fans.

> *Tobacco, tobacco,*
> *spit, spit, spit,*
> *if you ain't from Cincy*
> *you ain't worth shit*

Were we as full of Hudephol
everytime we applauded an Otis Nixon steal?
Were we as full of Leinenkugel
everytime we applauded a glorious balk?

There is no excuse for why grown men
would wear those tri-colored Expos hats,
not even shameful east-end haircuts
or faith. Why?

> *I went to Canada once*
> *bag of ice cost me two dollars*
> *no thank you*

Game One was a Cincinattian grandslam.
Game Two wasn't close at the start
and Game Three, heroically tied in the 9th,
was a big red stab to the heart.

> *I went to Canada once*
> *bag of ice cost me two dollars*
> *no thank you*

So we ran into the stadium's inner works
trying to get away from the rocket glare,
and outside we were just fine:
bought souvenir shirts that read *Free Pete*,
went for the chili five ways.
It was 93 degrees
and our hats were in our hands.

THE ALLIGATOR EXPERT PREPARES
TOURISTS FOR THE HUNT

The hinge of their lower jaws snap
arbitrarily, quick as a flame,
biting out when nothing is there.
It looks harmless at first,
like a birthday toy that will sputter
and break at your feet.
Its black and green triangular head
moves from side to side in a faulty rhythm:
a metronome gone awry.
Fabled to have gone after college girls' shanks,
to have left red semi-circles
in the bellies of sun-worshippers
from the central counties of Pennsylvania
and to have scared mothers worse than rubella.
At first the teeth look smooth,
lopsided pearls soft enough
for belly-button and dancing wear.
But the expert warns the group
the alligator's teeth are worse than any barracuda's,
descending from the tyrannosaurus rex —
sharp as machetes through Amazon shoots,
ready to fill the tourist roads of Florida
with eddies of blood and acres of bone shard.
They've been seen, hungry,
on the trim golf course greens
Ponce de Leon was looking for.

The alligator expert instructs tourists how to kill,
how to be as quick as possible
now the hunt has been declared legal.
He is armed with an aluminum stick
with a heavy charge at the end;

Poseidon's megawatt trident
charging order over the sea
and because of the sea, the land,
the bayous, swamps and everglades.
"You put the end of the stick
at the back of their heads,"
he says and notes the lichenous green
at that almost imperceptible curve,
"and you pull the trigger."
The alligator shivers out after the shock,
like a garden hose turned on full
after lying unused for months.
It all seems microwave efficient
to the group in sunglasses and extra-large t-shirts
looking for novel ways to spend vacation time.

He reminds them again and again
of the recent outbreaks and close calls,
of the jack-knives in their mouths
ready at any time to take away an extremity.
Like an old schoolteacher
he talks about their small brains
and the reasons why the dinosaurs
froze into the earth
and formed the gases and tar pits
in the subterranean blue;
about why the mammals rule,
why we are able to enjoy the Disney sunshine,
why we can inter their old bones
and mold them like greasy plasticine
in the neon of museums like state-funded art.
In the interest of avoiding
another alligator extinction crisis

the government has restricted the hunt
to night-time. At night,
when gator eyes skim up
above the black surface of the water
their corneas take on a reddish glow,
like bicycle reflectors
caught in the glare of an oncoming truck.
The glowing eyes are easy to spot
from the relaxed terraces of rented yachts.
The night-hunt has become a popular event
for bachelorette parties,
where the bride-to-be explodes the thing out of the water,
toasts her friends with sour rum drinks,
and walks down the gangway
with it over her shoulders: a garish stole
with swamp water trickling down her neck,
the deadened tail hanging over her breast,
a hardened orchid, football-helmet slick
and heavy as siamese babies.
Underneath the carapace of the tail
they say is something that can be sold
in the frozen food sections
of the supermarkets in America,
what with the fad for southern cuisine:
Blackened alligator, alligator étouffé,
alligator bienville, gator meat gumbo.
The expert says it "tastes like chicken"
even though he knows it doesn't.
It's a beefier kind of turtle meat,
chewy as molasses candy.
He shows off his ability to attract the gators
with a coloratura mating call.
Half birdsong, half whiskey murmur,

and the animal wags out of the marsh
and heads to the expert
in the hope of repeating the glory of eggs.
(Eggs that will be cracked
with probing beaks, or whose hatchlings
will dash into the warm swampland
where all disasters await.)
Not sure what to do next,
he shows the crowd how to dog and tie it:
he plays the tobacco-stained stampeder
for all it's worth, going "yee-hah"
as he binds the scissory mouth
with a kind of upholstery tape
and ties its rubbery black hands behind the back.

The crowd of tourists is awed
and wonders what anybody could do
with a full-grown captive alligator.
In Australia, an expensive hotel has an albino crocodile
entertain the guests by swimming around,
captive, in the outdoor lounge's pool.
The revival of the hunt, the expert sighs,
is mostly a search for revenge on the wolf.
There have been too many drunks
singing Jerry Lee Lewis songs to the beasts,
prompting them to snap at their grey shins.
Besides, the night-hunts could be something
along the ranks of spring break or Busch Gardens.
There is that dash of red
in the corners of the expert's eyes —
he's too tired to know what to do
about the tape around the jaw — he dreams
of some new test of their killer reputation
that has never been tried,
not all these humid nights, out on the glade.

CONFESSIONS OF A SOFTBALL BASTARD

I once beat the hell out of my best friend
Because he dropped a fly ball in short left;
I wish I could go back again to test
My wits — beat him harder and put an end
To the thought I may ever start to mend
The past, so send a note to the press
That bypasses my biceps and upsets
My art and my plan to never learn French.
I too sing a lazy kind of love:
For the next album I have a song called "Bone."
It's about this movie I sort of half-saw
(Fast-forwarded through — maybe with Rip Torn?)
Anyway it's about this guy and his dog
And they don't turn back and they don't turn back.

Spit, Robbie, Spit

Scratching and spitting, spitting and scratching;
they are as much a part of baseball
as cold hot dogs and warm beer.
(Except in Houston where tradition
is pretty much limited to losing and Frito-Pie.)
But my understanding was
players wouldn't spit on each other,
and, at least when the cameras were on,
they would try not to scratch each other.

They say the great Ted Williams once spit at the fans
and not even because of his idiotic nickname "Teddy Ballgame."
Basketballer Charles Barkley quite recently let a loogie fly
and the tale of this launch has become so finely distilled
I heard the acidity of his saliva blinded a Cub Scout
and destroyed *the faith of fifty million*
        potential souvenir cap purchasers.

So, Roberto Alomar, late of the fading Torontos,
and now doing his 5-million-dollars-a-year thing for the Baltimores,
spits at an umpire. That's the way it goes.
Stuff happens on the field — dirty, stupid, guy stuff.

Poor Robbie.
What good are the common people
        unless royalty can look down on them?

The ump missed the call!
Frankly, it's commendable Mr. Alomar refrained
from beating the blind idiot to death with a limp day-old calzone.

What happened to the once sweet and loveable,
dairy-board-promoting, putative author of *Second to None*?
Maybe it was the after-effects of so much tangy fruit punch.
Was it the 5% real juice or was it the 95% of the other stuff?
Maybe it's just a sign of the times, post-strike,
where baseball is like a millionaire's bowling tournament
except, of course, without the cool shirts and shoes
and with way more scratching and spitting.

But I still love watching the games
and seeing how it will all turn out.
I may complain
but I'm so dumb last year I spent close to $300
on Major League Baseball related products
and I live in Halifax, Nova Scotia.
Catch this:
I could turn away and just concentrate on reruns of *Full House*
but I'm one of *them*; a die-hard fan,
paying the way of all SkyDome Hotel residents
and waiting out disgust in the hope of another win.
As Gobbie Alomar himself said of the fans,
turning to Maryland
when Torontonians failed to show him the proper fealty,
"they had their chance."

KORDIC

Back then,
at the Hunter's Horn Tavern on Peel Street,
your name was mentioned
like a weather system,
terrible and new,
the evening of your first wild punch-up with the Habs,
your enthusiastic acceptance of your job —
"Don't you worry, eh,"
a man with monogrammed cuffs said,
"I tell ya that kid can really play."

But that was a different time,
a different Montreal.
Ste. Catherine street was enjoying its long collapse;
the stinks of The Tupper Tavern,
The Rymark, The Blue Angel and Diana's Dance Bar,
now somewhere faint in the corners of boarded-up businesses
on the long walk to the site of the old Forum.

In 1986 when the big silver prize
was paraded from Atwater to St. Lawrence,
your fistprints were all over it.
The street barely swept clear of broken window panes
faintly glittering at our feet like Hollywood *glassphalt*.
As famous as *Les Canadiens* were for winning,
Montreal had claimed an equally impressive reputation
for spectacular Stanley Cup riots.

Kiss your own knuckles:
another shift to say hello to Jay Miller,
another someone to dance with Marty McSorley,
another day at the office with Gord Donnelly.
You really could play the game,
like Wayne Gretzky or Frank Mahovolic
you were expendable in a timely trade.

Lost to the cold motel spaces of Quebec City,
lost to parents, lost to a fiancée,
lost to the language of the pro:
la claque,
Rambo, Hulk,
anabolic steroids, coke;
so, who feels bad, tough guy,
when cops put their knees between your shoulders?
when people you figure as friends
congratulate the cops on everything they've done?
Another bad example saved from the children of Canada,
more press for the narco-McCarthyism of the age
and the simple boundaries of a sports literature lunch:
it was OK for John Kordic to beat
the lights out of young Scott Walker,
but for John Kordic to have used cocaine was bad.

You were not the first man to die
under the knees of Quebec policemen
(Anthony Griffin, Martin Suazo, Marcellus François),
and you will not be the last.
Leaving the aches of the night
and interprovincial plane travel

Crescent Street is still bumping,
but the surroundings are closing in:
small mouse-eyes flashing
as the chase decelerates to evening's end,
failing to see one of our own in the bar glass,
and settling on the official line:
the failed *Kordique*,
la mort d'une brute.

4

QUINCY ON LYCIDAS

Anterior margins overlapping the front of the mediastinum;
wet and soggy lungs, jelly-like,
a glistening bluish-purple,
froth in the air passages,
water in the stomach,
hemorrhaging in the middle ear:
all signs are consistent with drowning, Sam.

But, Sam,
there's something's bothered me about this case
the moment the fat dingleberry's, I mean,
young swain's body was brought in,
two nights after being reported missing
from the deck of the pleasure craft *L'Eclipse*,
and thrown on my table like a ziplock sack of blue corn meal.
I saw something there — don't laugh, don't laugh, Sam —
maybe even a muted signal around his eyes,
downcast as if he wanted to avoid a photographer,
practically begging me to go further
and *yet once more* expose the secrets
of this corrupted county.

Drowning's hatefulness:
half-dreamed in teenage romance,
the vision of flailing out against the dark and enormous —
yet, thousands have managed the deed in the tub.
The body will never be one with the sea:
from head to toe we remain attached to our own particulars
and death offers no escape from *the blind fury*,
one-life-per-person, nothing perfect.

In the sea-washed bones of even the earliest settlers
you can always find the traces of tumors, toothaches,
sprains, hangnails, high blood pressure,
even clinical depression.

Last night, sitting on the deck of my houseboat,
watching airplanes touchdown at LAX,
the 747s were like lazy ducks gliding towards a soft lake,
beautifully, regardless of the blackness of night sky.
The air was calm and fragrant with summer.
Funny how nobody wants to go out in a plane crash,
in a quick overwhelming ball of gasoline flame;
no mementoes of even a second of trying to stay alive.
Looking at these confident jumbos
I thought about the wetter dream of disappearance,
slipping the hitch with a quart of white liquor,
wanting to scratch the moonlight on the waves,
to wreck the cheap porcelain muse,
to write forgettable little books of poetry,
to go around all important and puffy
telling you what the Buddha said
about earthquakes and haematomas —
I just can't go off like that.
I have a job to do.

He drowned, but did he just fall in? Jump in? Or what?
Sam, I had to snoop around.
Discovered he was an artist, or something,
and he'd fallen out with old friends,
fizzled with a recent flame,
dissolved a screenwriting partnership
with the author of an English-language
but still unbelievably pretentious play called *Les Americaines*,

and started making good money
(for once) writing ad copy and greeting cards.
Fame is the spur, they say,
and he went for it via the desirable 18-34 demo-share,
via the pocketbooks of those they despised (as college juniors).
I looked around and around and realized
he had his own line of cards
marketed carefully to those who think of themselves
as immune to Hallmarky sentiments —
you may have read some of the cutting-edge greetings:

> "Don't feel old . . .
> statistically you have at least five years
> before you die."

> "The best thing about you is . . .
> your hairpiece never clashes with your dentures."

> "Another birthday . . .
> another year listening to your crap."

Hardly gone a week, Sam,
people went out of their way to assure me he was "difficult,"
acquaintances biting their lips
reconstructing manic last days,
an implosion of *late show* griefs:
printing, but never getting to distribute an expensive series
due to their dark, unfriendly obtuseness:

> "What rhymes with Kevorkian? . . .
> Who cares!"

"Drop dead . . .
I'm serious!"

What his friends were up to, Sam, I don't know.
But it was more wine and liquidity for the aging hero
of a few overcrowded writing classes
at the Ventura Boulevard Screenwriting Academy,
killing as the canker to the rose,
stumbling into a Lava Lounge state of grace,
a deep-behind-the-cigarette personality,
a few L.A. losers *loved to hear his song.*

I went to see the alleged girlfriend anyway,
pretty as anything, an all-cotton Californian Amaryllis;
painting an antique chair on the sundeck,
her legs slung under a tarp protecting her lap,
her feet tapping quickly underneath.
She concentrated on her brushstrokes
while she calmly historicized the *hapless youth* —
she blew on the paint to help it dry quicker,
rubbed her eyes and admired the color.
"Butterscotch," she said, "couldn't you just eat it?"

She wasn't going to perform grief.
"You're in the death business," she said,
"sooner or later you must have shrugged-out
the graciousness of every hoary psalm,
and probably can't wait to go and get to the grog.
Look, Dr. Quincy,
I don't know a loon from a cormorant
and don't know the Italian word for health.
Tell me, what doesn't smell bad in this town?
What happens when the snake-head
of the loon or the cormorant
appears darkly, briefly, in your sky?"

So much for romance, Sam —
that chair wasn't fit for the Salvation Army showroom.
Have a nice night, I thought,
test your breath in your hands
while I test mine in the mirror.

Oh, she said all the things you might expect,
but through her *unexpressive nuptial song*
there was some muted regret curled in her hands,
stalled in the way she kept saying
"That's the way it is in Los Angeles."

Sunk low,
the algae in the stomach water
of a higher density, characteristic of greater depths,
as if he pushed himself to the Pacific floor —
but mounted high,
this punk who apparently cared for so little,
whose stomach was crammed with so much more
than the poisons swirling off Marina Del Rey.

Tell me, Sam, why a man who knew he was going
on a sea cruise would eat so much on shore?
Pink's chili dogs, Pollo Loco chicken legs,
Trader Vic's Mongolian ribs, Cassel's burgers,
Phillipe's french dip sandwiches, Central Market tacos —
the man went on a binge
that would shock Richard Simmons.
Why would he do that? What was so wrong
he'd take all that extra weight up the gangway?

I asked around everywhere and it was the same story, Sam,
always the same story, very defensive,
very secure in "how the hell should I know?"
or "what do you want from me?"

But *he must not float . . . unwept*
this dumb, plump, mini-Hasselhoff.
Back in the lab I double-checked the hemorrhaging of the ear
and probed deep in the eustachian tube.
When, suddenly, I saw a microscopic flash of chrome
glinting out like a silver nugget in a muddy sluice,
and I pulled it out with my microscopic tweezers —
a tiny metal capsule and inside of it
a piece of Japanese transfer paper
folded tightly, thousands of times over;
a small piece he wrote, monkishly inked there,
almost as if he knew
somebody just like me would read it.
Though I am not one to long sit and grieve,
O Tubby, *your sorrow is not dead.*

Let me read it out for you:

   all his beauty shed

      "rock w the waves" is sound advice
      but it doesn't account for the anchor tied to my foot,
      the chum in my pockets
      and the cpt who took me aside
      & whispered, "the love boat stops here"
      i still know what's underneath —
      they forget how much time i've been there
      and how much i remember about the details —
      the spiny fish, the charging eels, the sparkling minnows,
      the total embrace of the cold darkness,
      the loneliness, the absurd shortness of breath, saying
      "this is separate from my life up there"
      i shouldn't complain — i'm a bandit
      and i am lucky to have learned to spell "happiness"
      correctly once in my stupid life.

the dolphins tumble to the ocean floor
unable to breathe through new toxins
which have crusted the top of the sea —
the lobsters welcome us as derelicts
weighed to the very bottom by our maudlin faith
in hamburgers & poetry

r(egis)

santa monica, april 26 1996

Early detection is the key, Sam,
things written in the most prosaic notebooks
can metastasize like untreated cancers
and force an early goodbye.
Call him *the swart star*
the stout stud,
the stunted stoop,
or the surreptitious sandwich-man,
whatever.
There is no medical guarantee —
but there is one absolute certainty.

His words ringing in my head,
I went to see the old screenwriting partner,
a guy who followed the unsuccessful *Les Americaines*
with an equally unsuccessful play called *Partly Dressed*.
Stacking French photographic journals
about flowers and herbs, slowly,
stopping to take drags from a *Gitanes*
ever so delicately through his paint-stained fingers —
caramel écossais. The stagecrafter exhaled:
"He bid his fond *adieu*, Doctor Q,
with your new-fangled gore,
what do you want from me?

The croaks of the raven
and the deceptive coos of a thousand filthy pigeons?"

"Oh, I'll be seeing you," I said
and walked out to the evenings ahead.

Sam, who wouldn't want the sea to close in on them?
Sometimes I'd like to join that swim club
but, depressed, I catalogue and catalogue
and punch-in for work.
Dangerous chemical peels, over-the-counter amphetamines,
killer fad diets, paraquat, poisoned microphones,
there's always another reason to pick up the sword.
Sam, tonight, let's get together with Asten and Monahan
and wet down *the parching wind* at Danny's,
shouting *salute!* all through the stupid night.
Just months before the push, before the shove,
before the whatever, they called him
the genius of the shore.
Sam, he was murdered.

Letter to *tv* Guide

Dear *tv* *Guide*,

You can probably tell by my writing that I'm an old- fashioned person. So before you place this letter, the only one I've written in years, in your file of all dubious inquiries and nuthouse entrance exams, you should know I'm not writing to lament the disappearance of *Matlock* or to voice my support for Andy Rooney's latest unfortunate turn of phrase, or even to complain the orange juice these days "tastes funny." I'm not even sure how to put it. Like I said, it's been a long time.

After decades of working summers, cheese sandwich lunch breaks on a countertop with barely enough room for my elbows, sour-breathed overtimes with "hilarious" buyers who never want to buy, I've been downsized out of the marble-finished offices. But, inexplicably, I've remained a morning person, trying hard to fill-up on cranberry muffins one day, overindulging on french toast the next, handfuls of vitamin supplements bought on sale. And now I'm tuned-in to the indefatigable percolations of morning-tv.

I'm looking for a job but can't help but fall into my hands and laugh at the traffic reports. What was the deal with Katie and Bryant anyway? I'm asking you because my son was over the other day, gritting his teeth, tugging at his shirtsleeves, saying something to the effect that "they must be miserable" and Mr. Gumbel was wise to have moved out of "the land of smiles." I told Jason that was a nasty thing to say, but I was young once — just ask my barber. But I guess even my barber would say something decorous about "our lucky stars."

It's January now, all frozen spit on the sidewalk and McOatmeal mush caught in the bridgework of the employed, mumbling to their feet the poetry of how they just can't take it anymore. I can hear the mail-guy arrive and shake off the cold for the second he's in the lobby. Letters like this one never come around here, just financial statements. So let me put it this way: What's the use of putting on a brave face when the host of a morning show can't stand the pretense? Why is it I'm telling her "I'm looking, I'm looking"?

When she picks up Jason on Friday mornings she's just getting over her four-mile run and is trying her best to use some expression I'd never ever think of, like "high-carbo" or "agreed apportionment." And, please, don't think I'm that pathetic; it's been a long time since I wished she'd take the remote from my hand and tell me it's true, Babalu, and we'd rhumba the millennium away, all cigarettes, salsa and silk. She always ends up sounding like the firm's young bottom-liners who pointed me to the avenue, accompanying her exits with a low growl about how it's all about productivity; about seeing the big picture; and, if you're not careful, about a sausage-fed gang standing by an automatic teller, warming their hands, waiting to explain to you why God made them that way. I have no idea what she'd watch at home, probably those thoughtfully paced docu-dramas about the life-cycles of noble sierra animals, sun on their hides, slowly lapping at the edges of a great river.

We know how to talk to each other the way telephone company stooges talk to you about unpaid bills. And as far as Jason is concerned that's an improvement on our ridiculous attempts to "act like a family — just for a day." Anyway, I'm sure you don't really care about that and it's not why I've taken this fancy yellow paper out of the desk or why I'd like to talk to Bryant or Katie themselves. What about Matt? Even Willard, for God's sake. I can't make out like one of those bright midwesterners who stand around Rock-Center with signs that say *Des Moines Loves Today*. I just want to ask about those mornings, the ones where the grey sticks to the windows, when the ankles can't bear the pressure of the carpet, and when all your clothes scratch like straw. For sometime now it's been difficult to imagine a place that's not so quiet; even the Martian ice locked in the asteroids must make a substantial crack when it scrapes against the grit in the galactic atmosphere. So, my dear TV *Guide*, is there anyway I could get an address or a FAX number? Get back to me ASAP, and blessings to St. Jane, patron to all who get up for a reason. Just kidding really — look, I'm very, very happy.

Hawkeye is Dead

Dr. Dan scribbles on a prescription pad
"cross-border shoppers can kill too."
His son dropped seven years ago

in that little *gone-fishing* Maine town
with the picturesque wood shacks
everybody wants a postcard from.

His son had become "quiet," as they say,
unmarried, obsessed with distilled spirits, politics,
and the private sale of firearms.

Ever since he took a walk through the garden
of an Aroostook United Church
and claimed to see, through the pines,

the white stag nobody else sees
(except all the summer rentals who claim
to be working on a script for *The X-Files*).

Then he put together his bachelor hut,
muttering how he saw it, he saw it,
he saw it dart back into the woods

where it mockingly grows into a colossus;
antlers the size of oil company buildings,
blinding white haunches like iceberg tongues.

It wasn't long before he was selling stolen shanks,
black polymer Glocks, silver-plated .45s,
and a variety of field auto-shotguns.

Just seven years ago he was selling
an antique percussion wheelgun
that somehow went off and tore through everything.

The former pacifist doctor
and righteous chest-wound man,
unable to help himself, asked the bargain hunter

"Did you see him? Did you?
Take a look around and get him, get him."
It was ruled an accident.

The eulogies of nurses from Kaesong to Panmunjon —
well-intentioned commentaries about the peaceful
granite shores and the welcome silence of firearms.

But Dr. Dan says he remembers the early 60s
when they would get together in front of the TV
and complain about everything —

Dr. Dan spits a different color every day,
thinking, "My boy, I could have pickled him
and called him Abraham Lincoln Pickle —

O honest thing in a jar."

My Marilyn Munster

"What is *normal?*" you write in your daybook
after years of just smiling through the facts,
a path through the cobwebs of the house you grew up in,

off to football games, burger shops, and drive-ins;
taking home a cheque and wearily expressing love.
Now you see what *every day* can mean.

Maximum allowable insurance claims;
a variety of delicate cosmetic surgeries
fighting back a genetic code which frightens you,

married to a man who listens and understands —
even when you say all you want is to be somebody else.
And he takes his flakes and sings like Vic Damone:

"Who's the most beautiful girl in the world?
Oh, that's my very own Marilyn Munster."
So every now and then you call him "Tiger."

But the mirror shoots back Karloffian,
lycanthropic possibilities —
sometimes in the afternoon you just have to lie down.

You drift into warm overdue sleeps
where birds turn into bats and hands turn into claws
and the basement starts creaking with memories;

the forearms of the dragon that lives down there
smashing across the stacks of your boxed college books,
ripping your underlined copy of *The Cappadocian at Silene;*

the pallid tail swinging and whipping up the smell of fire,
floating ginger-breathed whispers
of places you'll never be, a fulfillment

beyond the refurbished bay windows sending you
to the pool of the *Creature from the Black Lagoon*
while hubby finances your sporty blue GEO.

You called the monster "Spot,"
and you fondly lace your aerobic shoes
to live the life of a happy, well-adjusted person:

Like your Uncle, folding your thick arms
somewhere near the sight of the television
to coldly watch the year tick down;

like your Aunt, striking that *poor little me* look,
waving away any suggestion of help
but coughing while you get your way.

It was *normal* to never say:
"Hey why are you people acting like drive-in movie ghouls?
Why do you feel sorry for me?"

You figure out the cruelties of the suburbs
as the world scatters from your smiles,
forgetting forever and, with a beauty that shocks God,

putting your pen on the dashboard
as you go to take out a sizable loan against the house,
to fight the unmistakable appearance of a fang.

NATALIE LOSES WEIGHT

"Did you get your haircut?"
"Is that a new outfit?"
"Is that Cher's new perfume?"

They have to say something stable
to reward your new comfort in economy cars,
but who can figure out the right words?

How to address the heavy topic?
Well, let me translate
so there's no confusion about the experience:

"Are you losing weight?" means *you fat pig*,
"How much weight did you lose?" means *you fat pig*,
and "Are you on a diet?" means *you fat pig*.

Yes I am. I'm not sure why;
it wasn't a moment of supreme disgust after diet candies
had melted on my precious copy of *Bat Out Of Hell*,

or that I once found myself in a drive-through before dinner,
singing "love will be my victory"
to the so-called sandwiches, the only thing without conditions.

You're such a *good* person, they say, but
how can you account for the neediness of a girl
whose first boyfriend was nicknamed "Snake"?

I feel like putting my diminishment into words
is as dumb as saying you "hate old people"
when applying for a job at Walgreens.

But what would I say to my old friends
who have their own struggles,
their own get-rich preludes to their discount soap?

Once I really cared about their gazelle accelerations
and leatherette apothegms,
now we are like everybody else.

What would I say besides "I didn't make it after all"?
Could I crank out some grand tale and whisper
of how I wasted my inheritance at the goat races in Tobago?

They'll see all this as my greatest accomplishment
but they really want the details,
the *John Candy's last meal* type details,

Himalyan stacks of mashed
and jumbo pizzas dealt with like raisins —
and, of course, without wine it's half a meal.

Tra-la-la-la-la-la-tribulations —
my wild dance is like a tango,
but it's something I never thought of sharing.

I'll take my answer behind the yellowgreen suburban shrubs,
behind the frosted glass tousle of a retro Farrah cut,
and mumble underneath the palliative redbird whistles.

A loneliness sweeter than any flavor of gelato
will fill me up as I get so thin
old rings will not stick to the knuckle;

finding paper ribbons for my life story
part varicose veins, part lucky number —
maybe we'll bump into each other on the street before lunch,

but with a case full of important diskettes
and appointments with guys named "Victor" and "Claude,"
I'm not that hungry anyway — maybe some other time.

5

Prayer for Selena (Agnus Dei)

Precious,

We're done. The doctors would have found something,
they always do,
but as I drive north again,
misunderstood
lyrics recorded in notebooks,
just trying to feel good enough to *see;*
there's no massage left in that bit of fatalism
you left too soon and everything feels stuck.

(Line-ups of mourners in south Texas
under thin branches of mesquite trees, dreaming of you.)

The English words held inside;
to ask where you were buried
seemed too obviously suicidal —
but I still asked about Room 158 at the Days Inn:
Tu Solo Tu.

T-shirt tsunamis, Elvisianna,
miracles of acceptance;
a velvet rope which separates you from us;
your vibrance, youth, and little miracles.
I'm back up (I think),
I'm alive (I hope).

Packing
recuerdos de aquel Brownsville
and back up to Quebec;
a good night's sleep at *La Dernière Auberge,*
right across the border.
Down-payments, cranberry for your health,
I don't care what they say —
this time I will successfully
run away from myself.

When the car is fighting against me
like some ferocious Gulf treasure,
and I'm cursing the odometer
and its doomed milestones,
when the air conditioner is jacked
cold as a Corpus Christi mall,
I leave my best with your gone voice
still charming the radio.

Precious,
I don't know how to drive.

State Line Road, Texarkana

The Exxon station attendant
doing his best with the metric system
looks around, mops his neck, and says
"You might as well take a walk or something,
this could take a-while."
It's been a bit since I said something out loud
besides "I'll have one of those,"
uncertain of what I can manage to make sense of
esp.
the words.
Left for dead in Dallas,
headed for Arkadelphia,
city of Arky love.
"A-OK" I say.

As he proceeds to tear the car apart,
I head for the KFC,
a 2-piece dinner to go
and behind the restaurant
it was like a cat darted between my feet
and I lost my balance and fell down a ravine,
tumbling through brambles and cardboard litter,
holding onto my chicken and biscuits for dear life.
There, at the bottom, motionless,
I wait for God to tell me to start digging,
to tell me, despite the occasional flashes,
I was always a little too disorganized,
a little too *off the top of my head*
to have sealed-up the fate of those who knew.
I imagine God putting in his contacts, squinting
to inspect the details of my coffin;
cow-headed, arms-folded,
his unimpressed stare as I descend,

his "You're not much of a grave-digger, are you?"
his "Once you're done, I won't be unhappy."
Shovelling down
until I barely can see anything except the night sky;
but that deep, I finally realize
he is less a God and more a corrupt ugly Cop,
like Sterling Hayden in *The Godfather*,
and I'm just hoping Sonny's taped the pistol to the tank
because I will finish the job.
I'll keep going but I'll know by the music,
all bald tires on the driveway, hyena laughs,
windtorn tarpaulin and shotgun kick-backs —
when it'll be my birthday,
a red letter day in my gift to myself,
A Druid's Agenda Book:
　　　　eat dirt,
　　　　worship a tree,
　　　　fear the sun.
I'm proud I held onto my lunch:
I enjoy every torn bit of chicken skin,
I rebuild my meticulous comb-over,
and think of something remorseful in a glass.

I'll be in the mood for it tonight,
after I've signed the postcards:
the vineyards of Northern Ohio,
the gunshops of the Florida panhandle,
the brandywines of Boston's financial district,
stealing time for grits and grillades on Canal Street in New Orleans,
buying a stolen watch on Canal Street in New York,
cracking my skull on the rink at Houston's Galleria mall,
spitting pepitos in a styrofoam cup in the San Bernardino shade,
Wisconsin butterburgers, Merrimack valley miniature golf,
angry barstoolers in Chicago, angry mosquitoes in Maryland,
the flooded truckstops of Iowa, Graceland on New Year's Eve,
and (by mistake) the so-called "dryest county in Kentucky."
One last batch of postcards and I am finished.

Cut and scratched,
I'm back on the street
the silver-swimsuited population of the billboard above
winks of light beer and relief up north,
all lakeside retreats and incredible custards.
No cool stops nearby,
I walk into that familiar superstore chain,
buy a U of Texas Longhorns jogging suit
and some Shaquille O'Neal Band-Aids.
Changed and fixed up,
I went and sat in the Windex-strafed cafeteria
to enjoy the cold of a 44oz. Diet Coke
before heading back to my last stand.
No friendly questions about my accent today, please,
I'm in the tunnel, eh, the tunnel, *allô*, the tunnel,
the walls covered in ectoplasmic horribleness
that chokes off before the end,
the light where the airport runway is —
leave it, leave it . . .
I traded everything I once knew
about Bartók's night music
for a goldbrown sweatsuit.
Fair enough,
but why the sucky regret?
Why the tequila shooter slogans,
the crowd-pleasing sitcomic jukebox
all b-sides stuck on Hank?
Mind your own business.
This is the long run,
the jumbo drink
I drink to the aspartame lees,
fuckface.

Then a cat — it was a cat —
a dirty alleycat wearing a dark kitty t-shirt,
jumped on the table, kicked the soda over
and went "fiddle die fee
you are the arsiest —
hey, so what if you've heard it before,
you are, you are, —
die now and now if you can't take a joke."

I don't know what they all did to that little car,
or how long it would last,
but it pulls into the center lane of the Interstate,
a bit faster than it should,
happy to feel that deep fried queasiness,
ready to hit every great state
from New Delaware to West Carolina
just to make up for lost time.

FOND DU LAC, WISCONSIN

At the Adler Planetarium in Chicago, Illinois
moon stones under plexiglass revealed nothing;
on the bus outside of Milwaukee, the Wisconsin countryside
could not overwhelm the turning half-thoughts,
the warping reflections in the windows, the rumbling.
I want everything to stop and spin backwards
to where I'm all ears and brushing back your hair;
I've been lonely but I've never been alone
and your familiarity with that place
is still beyond my skills as a navigator. What's there?
I know the food is terrible but some prefer it that way;
alone, nobody will ask you where you are (except me
again). It's not the past, the dullness
of rocks dragged back for show-and-tell which hurts,
it is the glimmer of the moon, its killing smirk,
its smoky indulgence of the earth's limitations —
there'll be a glimpse of Venus in the morning sky,
but to the moon now we'll share a homesick prayer:
never alone then, only with you and then, never lonely.

BURGER ON YEATS'S GRAVE

At dawn, near Dun Aengus on Inishmore
I had a vision:
I would put a hamburger on W.B. Yeats's grave.

A vision of opening up pale wax paper
in front of a sharp tombstone;
meaty and simple,
the unpretentious burger.

Then slumped on a Galway bus I would ride,
the p.a. playing so-called new country
full of polished regrets and absent of hangovers,
slowly curling through the west coast towns,
creeping surely to my destiny.
By the time I stepped out at Sligo Station
I phoned overseas again,
curious, if in my long absence,
the apartment had been burglarized.
Feeling a guilty swell about the pursuit,
the ground beef odyssey,
numbed by the slow drive,
by the staring out at the useless,
pretty furze of the countryside.

"When are you coming back?"

"Soon, beautiful."

The sandwich was bought on O'Connell Street
at an unfussy fryshack called *Fast Food*.
No cheese, Yeats might not approve —
going to the place where all burgers start?
The fresh belly-bomb tucked in a jacket pocket,
warm to the side, a whiff of mustard;
pedalling a rent-a-cycle out of town,
out to under Ben Bulben's head
just as a luxury tour bus creaked away.

The coffeeshop by the gravesite was empty
and groundskeepers milled about,
raking stones already
raked as much as stones could be;
by myself in the damp air
I left the still warm prayer and passed by.
I heard another tour bus sidling up,
full of good people in green Adidas track suits,
full of their own agendas to keep.
Would they see the burger as disrespect?
As garbage?
Would somebody from Seattle
pick it up for a comic pantomime nibble
and write a piece about it for the local press,
What's happened to us?
I was gone:
on a late night train to Dublin
full of uniformed school kids
so glad to be moving along,
reciting lines from their favorite shows.

QUINPOOL ROAD, HALIFAX

—for N & B

Waving goodbye again:
hearty, comic gestures over the hedgerows,
just enough to see;
fading behind the long white houses
whose promises are impossibles now,
whose signatures and guarantees
go well beyond the simple flourish of a pen;
those sitcomic expressions,
the evergreens and Christmases
unable to hold still, suddenly
walking towards something else.

Like any other small boulevard:
once the hope of renewal
but now the embrace of its own decline;
gyro-slicers and fast food women
still serve you with great smiles
and when that smile is not quite there
the complaints start coming,
even though it's understood
it's all just business and make-believe.

Televisions, sneakers, CDs, desk lamps:
anything you can get
you're better off getting at the mall.
Massages, donuts, cheques cashed:
it is impossible to measure how long it takes
to get from one end to the other.

Store fronts dropping:
an old grocery chain makes way
for a new healthfood chain
where the fantasies of control and vitality
are retroactively patronized;
the dream of escaping the bonds of place
collects its own proteins
in the reservoirs of *have a nice day*
and takes off confusedly
over the great waves of the ocean,
leaving behind old, soft affections:
ornamental dinner plates,
crowded bulletin boards,
too little money,
not enough time.

Sad restauranteurs
serving the same puddles of brown
to the same declarations:
This is the best I've ever had,
I love it more every single day;
prodigious video retailers availing all (and nothing)
from *Carrington* to *Strap-On Satisfaction;*
dependable dry cleaners
sorely needed
as the pigeons too
must sing their song.

The major intersection is full of threats
as high schoolers negotiate
their cigarettes and broken hearts
around the traffic lights;
a willow tree in the median
roots to where the telephone lines
and plumbing have worked for years
without ever thinking about how,
without having to battle
the determinations of the wild.

One hope flies to the planets again:
to Jupiter, whose thin, flat ring
circles clouds of ammonia ice;
meanwhile, the walking road
has its certainties;
east, to the workplace,
where it's all fresh cotton
and arms brushed against arms;
west, to the narrow inlet
where the water slips to the sea
and every dissoluable thought
mixes well with disappearance.

Taco Bell in Kingston

Fall colors steep in the backgrounds of Division Street
but through the restaurant window's tint
all the fading properties of chlorophyll are greyed;
the ochres, the oranges, the reds and the brown dusts
all cooled into the tones of used autoparts.

The odors of Cornwall, the quaintnesses of Brockville,
the coffee and chewing gum, the anticipations and regrets,
taking a break from all things to be silent about.
The maplewood and alfalfa,
the dairy farm cheese stores and orchard craft shops,
the treefarms and inland seagulls,
the coming October rains
spelled in another lineup, another modest hunger.

To get the meal officially associated with happiness,
the one with all the cool stuff inside,
you have to specifically order the kids' meal,
and no matter how nice the staff is,
how unproblematic the gesture would be,
we can't seem to bring ourselves to ask for one.

They play rock and roll music from the 1960s,
so much more disturbing than the great *3 M's of Muzak*
(Mantovani, Mauriat and Melachrino),
and much worse for all the parents singing along,
boring their kids with "Oh I remember this one;
don't you remember this one, honey?"
and their fussing with intense worry
whether the "Mexican french fries" will be "too hot."

We all need a little extra capsaicin.

You take your soft chicken taco
and I'll take my chicken burrito.
It's all good
and no surprise.
Whether it's your first time
or if you've been coming here for 14 years,
you never ask "how is it?"
It just is.

VILLE D'ANJOU IS HEAVEN TO ME

Minty fresh forever and us;
sunshines went some breakfast cereals ago,
but I gave and gave and get OK for winter
when the snow sugars (*legato*) the angles of the lawn.

Never leaving, never saying goodbye.
I'm looking toward a more forgiving diet,
but there's no need to explain to you how things really are,
for I have touched the four corners of the world:

from the narrow gardenpaths and ash trees of Talcy
to the dim lights and cubicles of Des Roseraies;
from the prairie view to the acetylene towers on Alexandre
to the icy grey steppes of Mont St. Antoine.

In some enchanted grotto I will find myself choking
but the chlorine,
the chlorine will bleach my hair —
I won't leave until somebody invents Kentucky Fried eggs.